D1710765

VAMPIRES IN FILM AND TELEVISION

Jennifer Bringle

rosen publishing's
rosen central

New York

To Rodney, my favorite horror movie fan

Published in 2012 by The Rosen Publishing Group, Inc.
29 East 21st Street, New York, NY 10010

Library of Congress Cataloging-in-Publication Data

Bringle, Jennifer.
Vampires in film and television / Jennifer Bringle. — 1st ed.
    p. cm. — (Vampires)
Includes bibliographical references and index.
ISBN 978-1-4488-1226-4 (library binding)
ISBN 978-1-4488-2229-4 (pbk.)
ISBN 978-1-4488-2236-2 (6-pack)
1. Vampire films—History and criticism—Juvenile literature. 2. Vampires on television—Juvenile literature. I. Title.
PN1995.9.V3B75 2012
791.43'675—dc22

                                                        2010018462

Manufactured in Malaysia

CPSIA Compliance Information: Batch #S11YA: For further information, contact Rosen Publishing, New York, New York, at 1-800-237-9932.

On the cover: Left: Robert Pattinson plays Edward Cullen in the Twilight saga. Right: Count Orlok was portrayed by actor Max Schreck in the silent film *Nosferatu*.

CONTENTS

INTRODUCTION

WITH the success of the Twilight books and films, and television shows such as *True Blood* and *The Vampire Diaries*, vampires in popular culture are hotter than ever. But long before Edward and Bella first met or Buffy slew her first vampire, these creatures of the night were an important part of movies and television shows.

During the early years of film, silent movies introduced audiences to the vampire. Using elaborate makeup, exaggerated movements, and strong facial expressions, silent film actors brought the horror and mystery of vampires to life. As sound was introduced to film, actors like Bela Lugosi gave vampires a voice and made them more popular than ever.

With the advent of television, vampires took on a more comic air with characters on shows such as *The Addams Family* and *The Munsters*. These vampires weren't fang-bearing monsters—they were joke-cracking comedians.

During the 1970s and 1980s, vampires in film became the stuff of cult classics and cheesy thrillers. Films such as *Blacula* during the 1970s introduced the African American vampire character. And 1980s'

movies such as *Fright Night* played up the cheesy, campy genre of vampire films.

But vampires have become a major part of teen culture in the modern era of film and television. With television series such as *Buffy the Vampire Slayer* and films such as *Twilight*, vampire movies and shows became a sensation among teens, and their popularity continues to grow.

But no matter what kind of vampire, or what the target audience may be, one thing's for certain—vampires always have been and always will be a major theme in film and television.

CHAPTER 1

SILENT VAMPS

LONG before Edward and Bella ever took to the screen, vampires were a major theme in moviemaking. During the early years of film, silent movies introduced viewing audiences to the bloodsucking creatures of the night. Taking their cues from literary works, filmmakers brought vampires to the screen, creating a horror staple that would endure to the present day.

LITERARY INFLUENCES ON FILM

From Count Dracula to Anne Rice to *Twilight*, the literary world has always had a major influence on film vampires. In the early days, works by Rudyard Kipling and Bram Stoker laid the foundation for vampires on-screen. And Stoker's *Dracula* is arguably the biggest influence on film and television portrayals of vampires. Stoker's tale is based on the story of Vlad III, prince of Walachia, more commonly known as Vlad the Impaler. Vlad received this nickname for killing thousands by impalement, or driving an object, usually a stake, through their midsections.

Published in 1897, Stoker's *Dracula* tells the story of the reclusive Count Dracula, who lives in a crumbling castle in a remote area of Transylvania. The count, who is really a vampire, aims to feed on the blood of innocent people. But Dracula is hunted by a group, led by Professor Abraham Van Helsing, who want to kill him.

These characters probably sound familiar, as they've shown up in countless movies and television shows throughout the years. By this century, Dracula has been the subject of more films than any other fictional character. One of the first and most controversial versions was the German film *Nosferatu*. Released in 1922, the film was an unlicensed version of Stoker's novel.

Stoker also wrote a short story called "Dracula's Guest," which loosely inspired the 1936 film *Dracula's Daughter*. It was released as part of a short-story collection in 1914, and some scholars have suggested it was actually a deleted chapter from the original Dracula novel. The story tells the tale of a man who gets caught in a storm and seeks shelter in a graveyard. He finds the grave of a countess who has become a vampire.

Another influence on vampire films has been *Carmilla*, by Sheridan Le Fanu. The gothic novel, published in 1872, tells the story of a young woman terrorized by a female vampire named Carmilla. This book became the inspiration for many female vampire characters in movies. One of the first to be influenced by the character of Carmilla was the 1932 Danish film *Vampyr*, which told several different vampire stories and featured a character named Carmilla.

One final, though not as commonly known, vampire film inspiration has been Rudyard Kipling's poem "The Vampire." Unlike *Dracula*, "The Vampire" isn't about a supernatural, bloodsucking monster. The poem tells the story of a woman who throws her man aside, breaking his heart.

THEDA BARA, FILM'S FIRST VAMP

Theda Bara was born Theodosia Goodman in 1885 in Cincinnati, Ohio. As a teen, Bara became interested in theater. Once she graduated from high school, she dyed her blond hair black and moved to New York to pursue her dream of acting.

Bara starred in her first play, *The Devil*, in 1908. During the next few years, she starred in several productions and acted in touring productions. Then in 1915, she got the role that would make her a star, the vamp in *A Fool There Was*.

During this time, the studio claimed her name, Theda Bara, was an anagram for "Arab Death." It also created a fake background, saying she was the daughter of an artist and an Arabian princess. Her notoriety grew, and she went on to star in several more films.

In 1919, Fox studios ended her contract, and she never returned to film. Instead, she chose to marry in 1921 and retire from film. She briefly returned to movies to appear in *Madame Mystery* in 1926. It was her last film.

Bara lived a fairly quiet life after that, opting to spend time with friends and family in New York and Los Angeles. She died in 1955, at the age of sixty-nine, of abdominal cancer. Though her films were made a century ago, she remains a legend in Hollywood to this day. She received a star on the Hollywood Walk of Fame in 1994, and her likeness appeared on a U.S. postage stamp in 1996.

Silent film star Theda Bara made a name for herself playing vamps in early films, such as *A Fool There Was*. In those days, a "vamp" was a woman who lured men, only to use them.

This theme of the female vampire, or "vamp," as a thoughtless woman who uses and hurts men was found in many early silent-era vampire films. One of the first of these vamp films was *The Vampire*, which was produced in 1913 and was based on Kipling's poem. In 1915, *A Fool There Was*, starring Theda Bara as the vamp, was released. The film takes its name from lines in the poem, which describe the man being used by the vamp. At the time, the film was considered very controversial for lines such as, "Kiss me, my fool!"

In modern times, vampire films have continued to be influenced by literary characters. During the 1990s, Anne Rice's vampire books spawned several movies, including 1994's *Interview with the Vampire: The Vampire*

Literary characters have always influenced vampire films. In modern times, books such as Anne Rice's *Interview with the Vampire* have been turned into popular movies.

Chronicles. The film and book tell the story of a vampire named Louis who lives in Louisiana after attaining immortality from a vampire named Lestat. The movie was a huge hit, starring many major actors such as Tom Cruise, Brad Pitt, and Kirsten Dunst, who played a child vampire. The final two novels in Rice's Vampire Chronicles series, *The Vampire Lestat* and *Queen of the Damned*, spawned the 2002 movie *Queen of the Damned*, starring R&B singer Aaliyah as Queen Akasha.

Probably one of the most popular literary-to-film vampire series of the modern era is Stephenie Meyer's Twilight saga. The book series, which includes four novels—*Twilight*, *New Moon*, *Eclipse*, and *Breaking Dawn*—has so far spawned two films, *Twilight* and *New Moon*. Films for all four books are in the works. The Twilight books and films tell the story of a mortal teenager, Bella, who falls in love with a vampire named Edward.

THE FIRST FILM VAMPIRES

During the early years of film, movies were silent, meaning there wasn't an accompanying audio track for the action on-screen. Some of these movies would be accompanied by music, but audience members never heard the actors' voices. That meant the actors had to work very hard to convey emotion and the personality of their character through facial expressions and other (often exaggerated) physical movements.

In vampire films of this era, actors had to rely on makeup, costumes, and strong facial expressions to show the horror of their character. In the film *Nosferatu*, Max Schreck played the vampire, Count Orlok. Using elaborate makeup (which is very impressive, particularly given the time period) and slow, menacing movements, Schreck portrayed one of film's

most terrifying monsters. Though the film was ordered destroyed after a lawsuit by Stoker's estate, copies survived and were restored, ensuring that the classic film endures.

During the silent era, vampire films were in their infancy. But with the advance of sound in films, vampire movies became more innovative and popular. The success of the sound films relied on the groundwork laid by these early film classics.

German actor Max Schreck played one of the first film vampires, Count Orlok, in 1922's *Nosferatu*. Because it was a silent film, Schreck relied on elaborate makeup and exaggerated movements to portray the monstrous character.

CHAPTER 2

VAMPIRES GO HOLLYWOOD: VAMPIRE FILMS AND TELEVISION DURING THE GOLDEN ERA

THE era of films from the mid-1930s to the 1960s is often thought of as the "golden era" of cinema. Many classic films were released during this era, and the actors and filmmakers gave off an air of glamour unseen since. During this era, vampire films also began to change and improve. The introduction of sound in film, and later, television, changed the way vampires were portrayed on-screen.

THE INTRODUCTION OF SOUND AND THE POPULARITY OF DRACULA

The introduction of sound to film was a major advancement in moviemaking. It also marked a major advance in vampire films. In the past, actors were dependent on makeup, facial expressions, and body movements to bring vampire characters to life on the big screen. But with sound, they could finally use their voices, and accents, to bring new horror and excitement to vampire films.

One of the first sound films to feature vampires was 1931's *Dracula*. The movie told the classic story of Count Dracula. It starred Bela Lugosi, who became famous for his portrayal of the count. Lugosi was a native of Hungary and grew up not far from the Transylvania border. His thick accent gave his depiction of the Transylvanian count an air of authenticity.

The film inspired a sequel, called *Dracula's Daughter*. The movie picks up where *Dracula* left off, telling the story of Dracula's daughter, Countess Marya Zaleska. The countess attempts to free herself of vampirism by burning her father's body, but it doesn't work. She is eventually killed at the end of the film by her servant, who shoots her through the heart with an arrow for going back on her promise to give him immortality.

Another sequel, *Son of Dracula*, came out in 1943. This film, starring Lon Chaney Jr., takes place in the United States, with the mysterious Hungarian Count Alucard ("Dracula" spelled backward) coming to the United States and marrying a woman in New Orleans. This film was notable for several reasons, including the fact that it was the first vampire movie to feature a vampire turning into a bat.

The film also marked one of the first major films starring Lon Chaney Jr., son of the silent film star Lon Chaney Sr. Chaney also starred in *House of Dracula* in 1945; instead of playing a vampire, he played the Wolfman.

These films, all produced by Universal Studios, set the studio up as the home for vampire movies. It continued to build on that reputation with two more films, 1944's *House of Frankenstein* and 1945's *House of Dracula*. Both starred John Carradine as Count Dracula.

Hungarian actor Bela Lugosi played Count Dracula in the 1931 film *Dracula*. The film was one of the first movies with sound, and Lugosi's accent helped make his portrayal legendary.

Dracula's popularity only grew throughout the golden era of film. A company based in England, Hammer Film Productions, released a series of vampire movies in the United States during the 1950s, 1960s, and 1970s.

The first of these was *Dracula*, renamed *The Horror of Dracula* for its American release to avoid confusion with Bela Lugosi's classic film. The movie starred Christopher Lee as Count Dracula. It differed a bit from the novel and the original film, omitting some events and moving others to different locations.

The film did fairly well and led to a number of sequels: *The Brides of Dracula* (1960); *Dracula: Prince of Darkness* (1966); *Dracula Has Risen from the Grave* (1968); *Taste the Blood of Dracula* (1969); *Scars of Dracula* (1970); *Dracula AD 1972* (1972); and *The Satanic Rites of Dracula* (1973). The sequels were all mostly released only in the United Kingdom.

The Hammer vampire films pushed the envelope with horror and gory special effects. In the years since, the films have achieved cult status, with many horror and vampire fans celebrating them as the gateway to modern vampire filmmaking.

VAMPIRES AND TELEVISION

During the 1950s, the new medium of television became popular in America. Before television, most people turned to movies and radio for amusement. But with television, families could have visual entertainment piped into their homes. During the early years, television shows were in black and white. With the advent of television's popularity came new ways to see and tell vampire stories. Several early television shows featured vampire characters, mostly in a comedic setting.

One of the first vampire television characters was Vampira, played by Maila Nurmi. Vampira hosted weekly horror movies and drew a cult following that landed her in national magazines and on major television shows.

One of the first television shows to feature a vampire character was *Vampira*. *Vampira* was a fairly groundbreaking show, as it featured a themed character hosting movies each week. It originally aired only on a local affiliate in Los Angeles, from April 1954 to April 1955. Although the show was only broadcast in Los Angeles, it was featured in national magazines such as *Newsweek*, *Life*, and *TV Guide*. Maila Nurmi, the show's star, appeared on several national shows such as Ed Sullivan's *Toast of the Town* and *The Red Skelton Show*.

FILM'S ORIGINAL DRACULA: BELA LUGOSI

Born in 1882 along the western border of Hungary, near Transylvania, Bela Lugosi seemed destined to play the legendary Transylvanian Count Dracula. By the 1900s, Lugosi was an established actor in Hungary, touring with the National Theater of Budapest.

When World War I began, Lugosi signed up to serve in the military. He fought on the Russian front and won the Hungarian equivalent of a Purple Heart. Due to his political activism, he was forced to leave Hungary in 1919 during the Hungarian Revolution. He went to several different countries before coming to the United States and becoming a citizen.

He began performing in New York theaters and was in several Broadway plays. Lugosi played Dracula in a Broadway production and was asked to take on the role in the film adaptation in 1931. With films just starting to use sound, Lugosi's version of the character was especially important because of his authentic accent.

Lugosi achieved great fame for his portrayal of Dracula. But he was typecast afterward, always finding himself offered horror roles. Lugosi's career faded, and he disappeared from film. He briefly returned in the 1950s when cult moviemaker Ed Wood asked him to appear in some of his films. Lugosi's last film was released in 1956, and he died later that year.

Although she was a gothic character, Vampira was more of a silent-era vamp than a movie-monster vampire. The character was based on the spooky *New Yorker* cartoons by Charles Addams, which later inspired the show *The Addams Family*. Vampira was similar to the Morticia Addams character from *The Addams Family*.

Another television show that featured vampire characters was *The Munsters*. The show premiered in 1964 and ran for two seasons, through 1966. It featured a typical family made up of the classic Universal Studios monster characters. The mother, Lily, played by Yvonne DeCarlo, and her father, Grandpa (also known as "Sam Dracula"), played by Al Lewis, were both vampires.

The Munsters was a hybrid of the classic family sitcom and the classic monster movie. The members of the family were all monsters, but they were also a regular family, living in a regular neighborhood. The show portrayed vampires in a humorous light, with the family getting into silly situations. It didn't include any of the darker themes often associated with vampires.

Although *The Munsters* lasted for only two seasons, it spawned several movies and a spin-off series. *Munster, Go Home!* premiered in 1966. The film, which featured the family traveling to England, was the first time the Munsters were seen in color. In 1981, a made-for-television movie called *The Munsters' Revenge* starred most of the original cast, including DeCarlo and Lewis as the vampire characters.

The Munsters spawned a spin-off series called *The Munsters Today*, which ran from 1988 to 1991. The show starred a new cast playing the original characters. The show took off from the story line that one of Grandpa's lab experiments put the family to sleep for twenty years, with them awakening in the late 1980s. The show used many of the original

In 1964, *The Munsters* debuted with a cast of characters that included two vampires—Lily Munster, played by Yvonne DeCarlo, and Grandpa (or "Sam Dracula"), played by Al Lewis.

show's props and story lines, including keeping both Lily and Grandpa as vampires.

Another popular show that featured vampire characters was the daytime soap opera *Dark Shadows*. *Dark Shadows* was on the air from 1966 to 1971. The show was notable as one of the first to feature supernatural characters. It also stood out because of its format—a daily soap opera. Most soap operas then, and today, are dramas that center on romantic relationships. While *Dark Shadows* had some of these dramatic elements, too, the addition of monsters as characters was nearly unheard of at the time.

One of the show's main characters was a vampire named Barnabas Collins. Collins was a centuries-old vampire searching for his lost love and, of course, fresh blood. The show and the character of Barnabas Collins became cult classics. Director Tim Burton, a fan of *Dark Shadows*, is reviving the series as a feature film.

The vampire movies and television shows during the golden era of film have served as inspiration for filmmakers and television producers even through today.

CHAPTER

3

SHOCK AND CHEESE: VAMPIRES IN FILM AND TELEVISION, 1970S–1980S

THE 1970s and 1980s ushered in a new era for vampire films and television shows. The two decades were filled with new interpretations of vampire characters. Filmmakers used new techniques and found new ways to tell vampire stories.

VAMPIRES IN THE 1970S

Continuing his rule as the dominant character in vampire film history, Dracula made a return to the screen during the 1970s. Two Dracula films were released during the decade. The first was a television movie in 1973, and the second was a feature film in 1979.

The 1973 version was a made-for-television adaptation of Bram Stoker's tale. It starred Jack Palance as Count Dracula. The movie deviated slightly from the novel's original plot. It included several plotlines that

In 1979, actor Frank Langella reprised his Broadway role of Count Dracula in a film version of the play. Legendary actor Laurence Olivier played Abraham Van Helsing in the film.

also appeared in the Barnabas Collins story on *Dark Shadows*, as well as elements that would appear in the 1992 film *Bram Stoker's Dracula*.

The film was produced and originally scheduled to air in 1973. But it was pre-empted by a speech by President Richard Nixon. Star Jack Palance was offered the opportunity to play the role of Dracula again after the film, but he refused. Palance was a method actor, which means someone who tries to fully inhabit and experience the character he or she is playing. He said playing the role was a little too intense for him.

The 1979 interpretation of *Dracula* starred Frank Langella as Count Dracula and legendary actor Laurence Olivier as Abraham Van Helsing. As in the 1931 version of the film, this one was also based on the stage adaptation of the novel. Langella played Dracula in the Broadway production that ran from 1977 to 1980. He was even nominated for a Tony Award for his performance.

Though the cast had impressive theater and film credentials, the film was only a modest success at the box office and was considered a disappointment by the studio. Critical reviews were mixed, with big-name reviewers such as Roger Ebert praising it, while others hated it.

Work by another literary master of horror, Stephen King, inspired a frightening vampire television miniseries. *Salem's Lot* aired as a two-part miniseries in 1979. The film was based on King's book of the same name and told the story of a town infested with vampires.

The film offered a significantly toned-down version of the book. Since it was a television film, much of the more graphic violence, as well as some social commentary, were minimized. The lead vampire character, though described as humanlike in the book, was made up in a monstrous fashion. In fact, his makeup and wardrobe were created to mimic that of Orlok from the classic film *Nosferatu*. The filmmakers wanted their vampire to exude evil and horror and not have a hint of the silliness that many vampire characters of the era had.

Salem's Lot drew big audiences and was considered both a critical and ratings success. It was even nominated for three Emmy Awards in 1980, including one for the elaborate makeup used in the film. It became a cult classic and served as inspiration for several vampire films in the 1980s, including *Fright Night* and *The Lost Boys*. *Salem's Lot* was also remade in 2004, starring Rob Lowe, Donald Sutherland, and Rutger Hauer. The miniseries was set in modern times, rather than the 1970s. The cast included several vampire film veterans such as Sutherland and Hauer, who both starred in the 1992 movie *Buffy the Vampire Slayer*.

Although these vampire films were serious interpretations of classic literary horror, another 1979 vampire film was a campy, comedic take. *Love at First Bite* featured '70s stars George Hamilton and Susan St. James as Count Dracula and Cindy Sondheim. Dracula believed Sondheim to be his reincarnated wife.

Set in modern times, *Love at First Bite* has Dracula coming to the United States after being driven from his castle in Communist Romania. He discovers inventions such as blood banks and falls in love with a fashion model, Cindy Sondheim. Sondheim's boyfriend, a descendant of Abraham Van Helsing, decides to destroy the vampire, but his methods fail. Dracula finally wins Sondheim over, and they marry and run away to Jamaica together, flying as bats.

Although *Love at First Bite* was very silly, it did well in theaters and was considered a success. There were several attempts to make a sequel, but none ever made it off the ground.

During the 1970s, a new genre of films called blaxploitation gained popularity. These were films aimed at African American audiences

WILLIAM MARSHALL: THE ORIGINAL AFRICAN AMERICAN VAMPIRE

Born in Gary, Indiana, in 1924, William Marshall became arguably the most famous African American vampire in film. As the title character in the blaxploitation films *Blacula* and *Scream Blacula Scream*, Marshall became a cult film icon. But beyond those films, Marshall had a long, diverse career.

After graduating college, Marshall moved to New York to train as an actor. He made his Broadway debut in *Carmen Jones* in 1944. He also worked as an understudy for fellow horror movie actor Boris Karloff in a production of *Peter Pan*. Marshall appeared in many stage productions, including several works by Shakespeare.

During the 1950s, he began acting in films. His roles were generally small, and he didn't achieve widespread notoriety for his film work until *Blacula*. During the 1980s, he appeared as a regular on the children's show *Pee-Wee's Playhouse*, playing the King of Cartoons.

In addition to his acting work, he also produced shows for PBS and taught acting at a number of colleges and theaters in California. Marshall died in 2003.

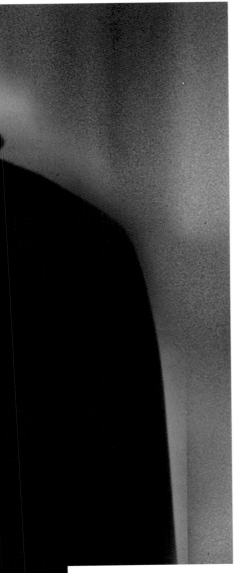

that often featured stories set in urban environments. Some people felt these films played on negative African American stereotypes.

Out of the blaxploitation genre came one of the first African American vampire portrayals, *Blacula* (1972). The movie starred William Marshall as a former African prince turned into a vampire by Count Dracula. Dracula imprisons Blacula in a coffin, which finds its way to Los Angeles nearly two centuries later.

The film wasn't a mainstream success, but it became a cult classic. However, it was still a financial success upon its release, and it even spawned a sequel, *Scream Blacula Scream*. The sequel was released in 1973 and again starred Marshall as Blacula. It also starred blaxploitation—and later mainstream—film star Pam Grier.

In the film, a voodoo queen resurrects Blacula to do her bidding. But he goes

During the 1970s, the first African American vampire portrayal hit the screen with 1972's *Blacula*. Actor William Marshall played the title role and reprised it in 1973's *Scream Blacula Scream*.

out on his own, terrorizing the city once more. He is eventually killed by Grier's character. Like its predecessor, *Scream Blacula Scream* also became a cult classic.

During the 1970s, vampire films and television explored new ground. From comedic interpretations to the first African American vampire characters, the decade's films made a lasting impression on the vampire film genre.

VAMPIRES IN THE 1980S

The comedic, tongue-in-cheek vampire movies of the 1970s carried over and thrived during the 1980s. The vampire films of the 1980s also laid the groundwork for the teen-centered vampire movies and shows that would become so popular during the next two decades.

One of the first of these films was *Fright Night*, which was released in 1985. The film told the story of a teenager named Charley who discovers his new next-door neighbor is a vampire. When a series of murders of young women occurs, Charley suspects his neighbor is responsible. But no one will believe him, so he turns to Peter Vincent, who hosts a late night horror show. Together, the two fight the vampire and kill him by exposing him to sunlight.

The film, which was one of the most successful horror movies of the year, featured a mostly teen cast. It also threw many jokes and comedic scenes in, which kept it from being as frightening as a traditional horror film.

Once Bitten, also released in 1985, starred a young Jim Carrey as a high school student being stalked by a female vampire, played by former model Lauren Hutton. Also a comedy featuring a teen cast, the film wasn't as big as *Fright Night* but has since become a bit of a cult classic.

CASSANDRA PETERSON: 1980S' VAMP

Like Theda Bara before her, Cassandra Peterson used makeup and costumes to create a classic vamp character. But Peterson wasn't always the vampy Elvira.

Peterson was born in 1951 in Manhattan, Kansas. After graduating from high school, she moved to Las Vegas and became a showgirl. In 1979, she joined the Los Angeles–based improvisational comedy troupe the Groundlings. A prestigious group that's spawned many famous comedians and actors, the Groundlings gave Peterson the chance to create the valley girl character that later became Elvira.

In 1981, she took on the show that was once *Fright Night*, turning it into *Elvira's Movie Macabre*. After her success with the show and movie, Elvira became a pop culture icon and one of the most famous vamp characters in history.

Peterson has appeared in many films and television shows, both as Elvira and as herself and other characters. She continues to appear in television and at events.

In 1987, two more memorable vampire films were released—*The Monster Squad* and *The Lost Boys*. *The Monster Squad* featured the classic movie monsters Frankenstein, the Wolfman, the Mummy, and the Gill-Man, led by Dracula. The story follows a group of kids who are fans of these monsters. They dub themselves the "Monster Squad." They find the diary of Abraham Van Helsing and translate it from its original German. The diary tells of a day of balance between good and evil, when evil (the monsters) can return and cause trouble. The kids work to prevent this from happening.

While *The Monster Squad* had modest success, *The Lost Boys* became a huge hit. It featured an all-star cast of some of the biggest teen/young adult actors of the time: Jason Patric, Kiefer Sutherland, Corey Feldman, Jami Gertz, and Corey Haim.

The film tells the story of two brothers (Patric and Haim) who move to California to live with their mother. The town they live

The Lost Boys, a teen-focused vampire film, was a huge hit in 1987. It starred some of the most popular teen stars of the day—Corey Feldman, Kiefer Sutherland, Corey Haim, and Jason Patric—as vampires and vampire hunters.

in is plagued with gangs and unexplained disappearances. The boys soon discover that a gang of teen vampires is responsible for the city's crime wave. The brothers get involved with the gang, one becoming a vampire, the other teaming up with two self-proclaimed vampire hunters to kill the vampires.

The Lost Boys was a big hit, making millions at the box office. Even though it was rated R, it drew large teen audiences due to the popularity of its stars. In 2008, a sequel, *Lost Boys: The Tribe*, was released. It starred original cast member Corey Feldman, with cameos by two other original cast members—Corey Haim and Jamison Newlander. It wasn't nearly as successful as the first film.

The success of *The Lost Boys* hinted at the future runaway popularity of vampire movies featuring teens. During the 1990s and subsequent decades, teen-focused vampire films and shows became instant hits.

Also during the 1980s, there was a resurgence of the original vamp character in the form of Elvira, Mistress of the Dark. Producers at a Los Angeles television station wanted to revive the themed character hosting B-movie horror films, like *Vampira* from the 1950s. Actress Cassandra Peterson responded to the casting call for the host and won the job. She styled her character, Elvira, after Vampira but with a twist. Like Vampira, Elvira was a vixen in a black dress. She wore heavy eye makeup and had long black hair. She also spoke with a valley girl accent, cracked jokes, and made fun of the movies she showed on her program.

Elvira's show, *Elvira's Movie Macabre*, first aired in 1981. It became so popular that it was syndicated and shown in cities across the country. Elvira appeared frequently on talk shows, such as *The Tonight Show* with Johnny Carson. She also had her own line of merchandise that included comic books, Halloween costumes, action figures, and calendars.

Her popularity led to a feature film, *Elvira, Mistress of the Dark*. The film was released in 1988. The movie finds Elvira losing her television job and moving to a small Massachusetts town after inheriting a house from a deceased aunt. Elvira's vamp image disturbs the residents of the conservative town, and they accuse her of being a witch.

Elvira's popularity continued through the 1980s and early 1990s. Her distinctive take on the classic vamp character introduced the concept of vamps to a new audience. And it helped ensure that all kinds of vampire/vamp characters would endure throughout the history of film and television.

CHAPTER
4

FROM *BUFFY* TO *TWILIGHT*: THE MODERN ERA OF VAMPIRES IN FILM AND TELEVISION

DURING the 1990s, vampires in film and television gained new popularity. Thanks to new ways of telling the vampire story, and creating vampire movies and shows that appeal to audiences beyond horror buffs, vampires became more popular than ever.

THE DAWN OF THE SLAYER

One of the first vampire slayers, Professor Abraham Van Helsing, was introduced in *Bram Stoker's Dracula*. But during the early 1990s, it was a perky blonde cheerleader named Buffy who became one of the most famous slayers in film and television. The movie *Buffy the Vampire Slayer* was released in 1992. It became a fairly huge success, especially among teenagers, and

A television spin-off of the 1992 movie, *Buffy the Vampire Slayer* featured a female vampire hunter played by Sarah Michelle Gellar. The show became very popular with both teens and adults, producing its own spin-off, *Angel*.

starred Kristy Swanson as Buffy. Buffy is a typical teenager until she is approached by a man who tells her she is the chosen one—the slayer. He trains her in the art of destroying vampires.

Buffy the Vampire Slayer was different from many traditional vampire films. Instead of being the victim or damsel in distress, the lead female character is the one who defeats the vampires. This made it especially popular among young girls, who enjoyed seeing a girl not unlike themselves as the hero in a movie.

In 1997, *Buffy the Vampire Slayer* came to the small screen as a popular television series on the WB network. The show was based on the movie and written by Joss Whedon, who wrote the movie's script. But the show was much darker than the film, and its story differed in many ways from the lighthearted movie.

The show starred Sarah Michelle Gellar as Buffy. Like her movie counterpart, the television Buffy is a high school girl chosen to be a slayer. But unlike the film, she's surrounded by a group of friends who aid her in her quest to destroy vampires. She also has a romance with a vampire named Angel, whom she's forced to slay.

Buffy the Vampire Slayer, the series, became a cult classic among both teens and adults. Its darker tone appealed to older audiences, while its youthful cast drew in teens. The show ran for seven seasons, through the spring of 2003.

Buffy the Vampire Slayer also spawned a spin-off series, *Angel*. The show starred David Boreanaz as Angel, who was the vampire love interest from *Buffy the Vampire Slayer*. Unlike most vampire characters, Angel wasn't evil. Although he'd done terrible things in the past, he felt strong guilt for his vampire ways and attempted to help others by working as a private detective.

TEENS AND VAMPIRES

While vampire films were mostly an adult genre during the first fifty to sixty years of filmmaking, in more recent times they've become the stuff of teen flicks. Starting in the 1980s, vampire films—and horror films in general—began featuring more teenage characters. Filmmakers and studios began making more and more of these kinds of films aimed at teen audiences. Long before the success of *Twilight*, young people flocked to the theaters to see such films as *The Lost Boys* and *Buffy the Vampire Slayer*. But what makes this such an attractive genre for young audiences?

Some film scholars and critics think the elements of adventure play a major role. Most teenagers and young people have limited freedom. Many have curfews and aren't allowed to go to certain places or do certain things that may put them in danger. But in these vampire films, the teens are the heroes. They take risks that ordinary kids wouldn't be able to.

Teens can also relate to the complicated romantic relationships that are usually part of these films. Often, human characters have difficult romances with vampire characters. By their very nature, they're pitted against each other, but love helps them overcome their differences, if only for a little while. Teen relationships are often very difficult as well, with pressures from peers and adults. So, teens often relate to characters on-screen who are also dealing with hardships in their relationships.

Angel was also quite popular, especially with *Buffy* fans. The show, which was even darker than its parent show, began in 1999 and ran for five seasons, until 2004.

In 1998, *Vampires*, starring James Woods, told the story of a team of vampire hunters. Directed by horror movie veteran John Carpenter, the film follows a group of hunters dispatched by the Catholic Church who are trying to prevent a centuries-old cross from falling into the hands of a master vampire.

Another popular vampire slayer in films was Blade. Loosely based on a Marvel Comics character, Blade first appeared in the self-titled movie, *Blade*, in 1998. The film, starring Wesley Snipes as the title character, tells the story of a half-human, half-vampire who protects humans against vampires. He works to destroy a legion of vampires living underground in the city.

Blade was so successful that it spawned two sequels, *Blade II*, released in 2002, and *Blade: Trinity*, released in 2004. Snipes reprised his character for both sequels. *Blade* also inspired a short-lived television series, *Blade: The Series*, which ran for a season during 2006 on the Spike network. The television show picked up where the story of *Blade: Trinity* left off. Snipes did not star in the show, though, so the character was played by hip-hop artist Kirk "Sticky Fingaz" Jones. Though it was the most-watched original series premiere on Spike, it was canceled in September 2006.

The most famous vampire slayer, Professor Abraham Van Helsing, returned to popular film in *Bram Stoker's Dracula* in 1992. The film starred Sir Anthony Hopkins as Van Helsing, Gary Oldman as Count Dracula, Winona Ryder as Mina Harker, and Keanu Reeves as Jonathan Harker. Famed director Francis Ford Coppola directed the film, which was based

In 2004, Hugh Jackman starred as Bram Stoker's famed vampire hunter, Abraham Van Helsing, in *Van Helsing*. The movie was the latest in the growing number of vampire killer–themed films.

on the classic novel. The film was popular with both audiences and critics alike and won Academy Awards for the elaborate makeup and costumes used to bring the characters to life.

Professor Abraham Van Helsing returned to film again in 2004's *Van Helsing*. This film starred Hugh Jackman as the famous vampire killer from *Dracula*. The movie also includes the character of Frankenstein's monster, whom Dracula attempts to force into helping him bring his undead children to life. In the film, Van Helsing tries to destroy Dracula, succeeding in the end.

ANNE RICE ON FILM

Like Bram Stoker, Anne Rice became famous by writing about vampires. The New Orleans writer penned several gothic novels featuring vampire characters. Her most famous, *Interview with the Vampire*, was made into the film *Interview with the Vampire: The Vampire Chronicles* in 1994. *Interview with the Vampire* was the first in a three-book series featuring the character Lestat. The film starred Brad Pitt as the vampire Louis, who was given immortality by the vampire Lestat, played by Tom Cruise. Louis tells his story in the form of an interview with a reporter, played by Christian Slater, during the 1980s. Louis resists his vampire tendencies, refusing to kill humans. He finally gives in and then tries to commit suicide, only to have Lestat save him.

Louis eventually bites a young girl, played by Kirsten Dunst, and Lestat turns her into a vampire daughter for Louis. The two attempt to kill Lestat but fail. Ultimately, Dunst's character is killed, and Louis returns to New Orleans, where he finds a weakened Lestat still living.

Lestat de Lioncourt is one of Anne Rice's most recognizable characters, appearing in the ten books of the Vampire Chronicles series. The series has sold around eighty million copies worldwide.

The film was a huge box-office success and was also popular with critics. *Interview with the Vampire* was also Kirsten Dunst's breakthrough film. Rice wrote the screenplay for the film, which was a close reflection of her novel.

The second film adaptation of Rice's Vampire Chronicles series was *Queen of the Damned*, released in 2002. Taking the name of the third book in Rice's series, the film used elements from both the second and third books. It starred Stuart Townsend as the vampire Lestat and R&B singer Aaliyah as Queen Akasha, the title character.

In the movie, the vampire Lestat is awakened by the music of a rock band. He then finds the band and becomes its lead singer, which angers other vampires. His music also awakens the vampire queen Akasha, who he ends up killing.

Rice was initially unhappy with the movie's production, since it didn't include key plot points from the second Vampire Chronicles novel, *The Vampire Lestat*. Her opinion of the film eventually mellowed, but most critics shared her original negative assessment: they panned the film. It fared better with audiences, topping the box office for several weeks. Many thought this was due to the fact that the film's star, Aaliyah, died in a plane crash in 2001, just months before the film's release.

Rice's film adaptations are some of the most popular and highest-grossing vampire films of all time. Her fans remain a loyal group, making the movies based on her books wildly popular.

MODERN VAMPIRE HORROR

During recent years, huge film budgets and the growing popularity of computer-generated animation have changed filmmaking. These developments have allowed filmmakers to create elaborate and terrifying new vampire films.

During the 1990s, films with larger budgets and better special effects became the norm. One of the first vampire films to benefit from this was *From Dusk Till Dawn*. Written by Quentin Tarantino and directed by Robert Rodriguez, the movie starred George Clooney, Salma Hayek, Harvey Keitel, and Juliette Lewis. The film combined two genres—gangster films and vampire films—into one movie. What begins as a film about bank robbers turns into a vampire horror film after the thieves on the run encounter the bloodthirsty creatures.

In 2007, two films featured vampire themes and had major budgets and dramatic special effects. One of those films, *30 Days of Night*, was based on a comic book series of the same name. Set in Barrow, Alaska, the movie tells the tale of a town overrun with vampires during its annual thirty-day period without sunlight. The film used special effects to help create the terrifying creatures that stalk this tiny town. Adding to the horror, special effects enhanced the gore level of fight scenes. The visuals, though amazingly realistic at times, make the film a bit too violent for younger viewers.

I Am Legend, which starred Will Smith, was a very different kind of vampire film. It tells the story of an experimental cancer cure that goes wrong, turning people into bloodthirsty, nocturnal, undead creatures. The monsters in this film are sort of a zombie/vampire hybrid, and special effects make them even more frightening. Like *30 Days of Night*, some of the visuals in *I Am Legend* are a bit too graphic for younger audiences.

The film also incorporated elaborate special effects to create an empty New York City. Since most of the city's population was killed or in hiding during the day, the filmmakers had to create a ghost town covered

in plants and grasses. They spent $40 million on models, sets, and computer animation to create the effect.

THE MODERN ERA OF VAMPIRE FILMS

During the last few years, vampires have become more popular than ever in film and television. Films such as *Twilight* and shows such as *The Vampire Diaries* and *True Blood* have all become major hits.

Many say that the recent vampire craze began with Stephenie Meyer's Twilight series. The books tell the story of a teenager named Isabella Swan— Bella—who has a complicated romantic relationship with Edward Cullen, a vampire who is more than one hundred years old. The four-book series became a runaway success with both teens and adults.

In 2008, the first film of the series, *Twilight*, was released. It starred Robert

Modern vampire films, such as 2007's *30 Days of Night*, use dramatic makeup and digitally enhanced and computer-generated special effects to up the horror factor.

Based on Stephenie Meyer's best-selling series, the Twilight films have made the vampire genre hotter than ever. Teens and adults thrill at the troubled love affair between mortal Bella and the vampire Edward.

Pattinson as Edward and Kristen Stewart as Bella. The story continues the classic vampire theme of one of the undead having a complicated relationship with a human.

While wildly popular and successful at the box office, *Twilight* had its fair share of critics. Many fans of the book were disappointed that it didn't follow the book as closely as they would have liked. But since the book was more than five hundred pages long, it would have been difficult to carry every bit of it over to the film. Fans of traditional vampire stories also found fault with the film because it broke many rules of vampire lore. In the movie, Edward and other vampires are able to withstand sunlight, which in traditional vampire stories meant death to the creatures of the night. Film critics also mostly panned the movie.

The film's sequel, *New Moon*, was released in 2009. In the second film, based on Meyer's second book, Edward and Bella are forced to split, and Bella becomes friends with a new boy, Jacob. She later discovers that Jacob is a werewolf—the age-old enemy of vampires. This further complicates her relationship with Edward.

New Moon introduced new actors, including Taylor Lautner, who played Jacob. Upon the release of the film, many advertising campaigns played up the rivalry between Pattinson's and Lautner's characters with "Team Edward" and "Team Jacob" merchandise. Both actors gained even greater status as teen idols.

The film was a huge success, bringing in major box-office numbers with its midnight opening. But like its predecessor, *New Moon* was mostly critically panned.

With the success of *Twilight* came a number of other vampire-themed movies and television shows. Two of the most popular are the shows *The Vampire Diaries* and *True Blood*.

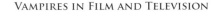

STEPHENIE MEYER: CREATOR OF *TWILIGHT*

Stay-at-home mother Stephenie Meyer never realized how much a simple dream could change her life. Meyer awoke one morning in 2003 after having a very vivid dream featuring characters she just couldn't get out of her head.

Meyer continued to think about the characters and began to work out a plot. Although she was busy during the day with her children and family, Meyer found time to write about these characters at night. After three months, Meyer finished her first novel for young adults, *Twilight*. She began shopping the book to agents, and it was eventually picked up and published in 2005.

Twilight became a huge success and spent twenty-five weeks in the number-one spot on the *New York Times* best-seller list. Meyer released the sequel, *New Moon*, in 2006 and its follow-up, *Eclipse*, in 2007. The final book of the Twilight series, *Breaking Dawn*, was released in 2008. All the other books in the series were also huge hits.

In 2008, Meyer released *The Host*, her first novel for adults. Like the Twilight books, it also became a runaway success. For Meyer, becoming a best-selling author and film inspiration was literally a dream come true.

Based on the book series of the same name by L. J. Smith, *The Vampire Diaries* premiered in 2009. It also mostly centers around teen characters—some vampires, some humans. Created by Kevin Williamson, who also created the *Dawson's Creek* television show and the *Scream* films, the show exhibits the same sharp-witted teen characters his previous works were known for.

True Blood is a much darker show and is for an adult audience. The show is based on the Southern Vampire Mysteries book series, and it premiered in 2008. It tells the story of vampires and humans coexisting in a fictional Louisiana town called Bon Temps. *True Blood* has become very popular.

These shows are just a part of the growing trend of vampires in film and television. As the genre has evolved over the years, it has drawn in wider audiences, ensuring that vampires will continue to be a strong theme in film and television for years to come.

1897

Bram Stoker's *Dracula* is published. It will go on to inspire countless films and television shows.

1915

A Fool There Was is released. It stars Theda Bara as the vamp.

1922

The German film *Nosferatu* is released. It is one of the first vampire films.

1931

Dracula, starring Bela Lugosi, is released. It is one of the first vampire films with sound.

1954

Vampira becomes one of the first television shows to feature a vamp character.

1964

The Munsters becomes one of the first prime-time television shows to feature vampire characters.

1972

Blacula is released, featuring one of the first African American vampire characters.

1979

The miniseries *Salem's Lot*, based on the Stephen King vampire novel, airs.

1981

Elvira's Movie Macabre begins airing, starring Cassandra Peterson as the vamp Elvira.

1987

The Lost Boys, a vampire film featuring an all-star, mostly teen cast, is released.

1992

Buffy the Vampire Slayer, which tells the story of a teen girl chosen to slay vampires, is released.

1994

Interview with the Vampire: The Vampire Chronicles, based on the Anne Rice novel, is released.

1997

Buffy the Vampire Slayer, the series, premieres on the WB network.

2005

Stephenie Meyer's novel *Twilight* is published.

2008

The film version of *Twilight* is released, starring Robert Pattinson and Kristen Stewart. It becomes a huge success.

2010

Eclipse, the third movie in the *Twilight* series, is released.

GLOSSARY

blaxploitation A genre of films popular during the 1970s that featured primarily African American characters and actors. Some say these films also played on racial stereotypes.

CGI Computer-generated imagery, or the use of computer graphics to create special effects in films.

cult classic A film or show with a small but very devoted following. These are usually films that don't do well with mainstream audiences or get negative critical reviews.

Dracula The title character of Bram Stoker's classic novel and the subject of many films and television shows. Dracula was a Transylvanian count who also happened to be a vampire.

gothic A style of fiction characterized by dark, mysterious circumstances.

horror A feeling of painful or intense fear; having the ability to induce intense fear.

immortality The state of living an unending existence.

macabre Describes a show, book, or other work having death as all or part of its subject; having a tendency to produce a reaction of horror.

silent film A film from the early era of movies that did not have an audio track accompanying the visual film. Many of these films were accompanied by music to set the mood and included title cards to add dialogue or set the scene.

slayer One who hunts and kills vampires in vampire films, shows, and books.

supernatural Relating to existence beyond the visible universe, sometimes attributed to ghosts or other dark or mythical creatures.

valley girl A stereotypical character meant to depict a middle-class or upper-class white girl living in the San Fernando Valley of California. The character is often distinguished by a distinctive way of speaking and dressing, usually in expensive and trendy clothing.

vamp A woman who uses her beauty to lure men for her personal gain. This type was first mentioned in a poem by Rudyard Kipling called "The Vampire" and later became a common character in film and television.

vampire A creature that is immortal and survives by drinking the blood of living beings. Vampires are night-dwelling creatures, as sunlight will destroy them. Garlic, crucifixes, and wooden stakes are also used to kill them.

Academy of Motion Picture Arts and Sciences

8949 Wilshire Boulevard

Beverly Hills, CA 90211

(310) 247-3000

Web site: http://www.oscars.org

The Academy of Motion Picture Arts and Sciences presents the Academy Awards. It also provides education and research about film history and preservation of historic films.

Berkeley Art Museum and Pacific Film Archive

2625 Durant Avenue, #2250

Berkeley, CA 94720

(510) 642-0808

Web site: http://www.bampfa.berkeley.edu

The Berkeley Art Museum and Pacific Film Archive is part of the University of California, Berkeley. The museum celebrates and educates the public about film history.

Buffy the Vampire Slayer Fan Club

VIP Fan Clubs

424 Fort Hill Drive, Suite 128

Naperville, IL 60540

Web site: http://www.thebuffyfanclub.com

A club for fans of the *Buffy the Vampire Slayer* television series.

Canadian Film and Television Production Association

151 Slater Street, Suite 902

Ottawa, ON K1P 5H3

Canada

(613) 233-1444

Web site: http://www.cftpa.ca

The Canadian Film and Television Production Association works to pro-mote and support film production in Canada.

George Eastman House
International Museum of Photography and Film

900 East Avenue

Rochester, NY 14607

(585) 271-3361

Web site: http://www.eastmanhouse.org

This educational museum works to tell the history of photography and motion pictures.

Museum of Broadcast Communications

676 North LaSalle Street, Suite 424

Chicago, IL 60654

(312) 245-8200

Web site: http://www.museum.tv

The mission of the Museum of Broadcast Communications is to collect, preserve, and present historic and contemporary radio and television content, as well as educate, inform, and entertain the public through its archives, public programs, screenings, exhibits, publications, and online access to its resources.

National Film Board of Canada

Norman-McLaren Building

3155, Côte-de-Liesse Road

Saint-Laurent, QC H4N 2N4

Canada

(800) 267-7710

Web site: http://www.nfb.ca

The National Film Board of Canada produces and promotes film in Canada. It offers educational information about Canadian film.

WEB SITES

Due to the changing nature of Internet links, Rosen Publishing has developed an online list of Web sites related to the subject of this book. This site is updated regularly. Please use this link to access the list:

http://www.rosenlinks.com/vamp/vift

FOR FURTHER READING

Bane, Theresa. *Encyclopedia of Vampire Mythology*. Jefferson, NC: McFarland and Company, 2010.

Bartlett, Wayne, and Flavia Idriceanu. *Legends of Blood: The Vampire in History and Myth*. Santa Barbara, CA: Greenwood Publishing, 2006.

Curran, Bob, and Ian Daniels. *Encyclopedia of the Undead: A Field Guide to the Creatures That Cannot Rest in Peace*. Pompton Plains, NJ: Career Press, 2006.

Curran, Bob, and Ian Daniels. *Vampires: A Field Guide to the Creatures That Stalk the Night*. Pompton Plains, NJ: Career Press, 2005.

Dashman, Josi. *Supernatural Girls* (Get the Scoop). New York, NY: Price Stern Sloan, 2009.

Dundes, Alan. *The Vampire*. Madison, WI: University of Wisconsin Press, 2009.

Goldberg, Enid A., and Norman Itzkowitz. *Vlad the Impaler: The Real Count Dracula*. New York, NY: Scholastic, 2007.

Guiley, Rosemary Ellen, and Jeanne K. Youngson. *The Encyclopedia of Vampires, Werewolves, and Other Monsters*. New York, NY: Checkmark Books, 2004.

Havens, Candace. *Joss Whedon: The Genius Behind Buffy*. Dallas, TX: BenBella Books, 2003.

Irvine, Alex, and Eric Kripke. *The Supernatural Book of Monsters, Spirits, Demons, and Ghouls*. New York, NY: HarperCollins, 2007.

Jenkins, Mark Collins. *Vampire Forensics: Uncovering the Origins of an Enduring Legend*. Washington, DC: National Geographic Society, 2010.

King, Stephen. *Stephen King Goes to the Movies*. New York, NY: Simon & Schuster, 2009.

Lecouteux, Claude. *The Secret History of Vampires: Their Multiple Forms and Hidden Purposes*. Rochester, VT: Inner Traditions, 2010.

Meyer, Stephenie. *Breaking Dawn*. New York, NY: Little, Brown Books for Young Readers, 2008.

Meyer, Stephenie. *Eclipse*. New York, NY: Little, Brown Books for Young Readers, 2007.

Meyer, Stephenie. *New Moon*. New York, NY: Little, Brown Books for Young Readers, 2006.

Meyer, Stephenie. *Twilight*. New York, NY: Little, Brown Books for Young Readers, 2005.

Mezrich, Vlad. *The Vampire Is Just Not That into You*. New York, NY: Scholastic, 2009.

Reinhart, Matthew, and Robert Sabuda. *Encyclopedia Mythologica*. Cambridge, MA: Candlewick, 2008.

Smith, L. J. *The Vampire Diaries: The Awakening*. New York, NY: HarperTeen, 2009.

Smith, L. J. *The Vampire Diaries: The Fury and Dark Reunion*. New York, NY: HarperTeen, 2007.

Smith, L. J. *The Vampire Diaries: The Struggle*. New York, NY: HarperTeen, 2009.

Stevenson, Jay. *The Complete Idiot's Guide to Vampires*. New York, NY: Penguin, 2009.

Stoker, Bram, and Zamorsky, Tamia, ed. *Classic Starts: Dracula*. New York, NY: Sterling Publishing, 2007.

BIBLIOGRAPHY

Elvira: Mistress of the Dark Official Web site. "About: Elvira, About: Cassandra Peterson." Retrieved January 10, 2010 (http://elvira. homestead.com/about.html).

Internet Movie Database. "The Lost Boys." Retrieved January 10, 2010 (http://www.imdb.com/title/tt0093437).

Internet Movie Database. "Theda Bara Biography." Retrieved January 10, 2010 (http://www.imdb.com/name/nm0000847).

Internet Movie Database. "William Marshall Biography." Retrieved January 10, 2010 (http://www.imdb.com/name/nm0551234).

Kane, Tim. *The Changing Vampire of Film and Television*. Jefferson, NC: McFarland & Company, Inc., 2006.

Karg, Barb, Arjean Spaite, and Rick Sutherland. *The Everything Vampire Book: From Vlad the Impaler to the Vampire Lestat—A History of Vampires in Literature, Film, and Legend*. Cincinnati, OH: Adams Media, 2009.

Lugosi.com. "Bela Lugosi Biography." Bela Lugosi Web site. Retrieved January 10, 2010 (http://www.lugosi.com/biography.html).

Meyer, Stephenie. "Stephenie Meyer: Bio." Stephenie Meyer Official Web site. Retrieved January 10, 2010 (http://www.stepheniemeyer.com/ bio.html).

Rice, Anne. "The Vampire Chronicles." Anne Rice Web site. Retrieved January 10, 2010 (http://www.annerice.com/Bookshelf-VampireChronicles.html).

Silver, Alain, and James Ursini. *The Vampire Film: From Nosferatu to Bram Stoker's Dracula*. New York, NY: Limelight Editions, 2004.

INDEX

ABOUT THE AUTHOR

Jennifer Bringle grew up watching vampire movies during the 1980s and 1990s, just as teen vampire films and shows were really taking off. In addition to this book, she's written several books for young adults about a number of topics. She lives and works in North Carolina.

PHOTO CREDITS

Cover (left) Eamonn McCormack/WireImage/Getty Images; cover (right) Frederick Lewis/Hulton Archive/Getty Images; pp. 9, 12–13, 18 Hulton Archive/Getty Images; p. 10 Newscom; p. 16 Universal Pictures/ Archive Photos/Getty Images; p. 21 CBS Photo Archive/Getty Images; pp. 24 Mary Evans/Ronald Grant/Everett Collection; pp. 28–29, 46–47 apaphotos/Newscom; pp. 32–33 Jane O'Neal/Warner Bros./Getty Images; p. 37 Getty Images; p. 41 © Universal/Everett Collection; p. 43 Mary Evans/Geffen Pictures/Ronald Grant/Everett Collection; p. 48 Photoshot/Everett Collection; interior graphics (bats) adapted from Shutterstock.com.

Designer: Les Kanturek; Editor: Bethany Bryan; Photo Researcher: Peter Tomlinson